CW00553098

MONARCH OF THE ROAD

A CELEBRATION OF A LONDON ICON

First published 2007

ISBN 1-906311-00-5

Published by Routemaster Operators & Owners Association

Compiled by Andrew Morgan and George Watson

Designed and produced by Creative Art & Design
www.caduk.net

Printed by XpressLitho
Tower Road
Washington
Tyne & Wear

www.routemaster.org.uk

1. INTRODUCTION

July 2004 witnessed a possible unrepeatable event in the history of London's buses.

Over 100 of London's famous Routemaster buses joined in to celebrate the 50th birthday of the first RM1, being unveiled in the Summer of 1954.

Most of these gathered in Finsbury Park in north London for the unique two day event, whilst the others ran on public services across London.

This publication provides a photographic record of some of the significant and memorable aspects of that special weekend; a tribute to a vehicle which is so much an icon of London and who's story is still far from over.

Each vehicle entrant that attended the event at Finsbury Park received a brass rally plaque.

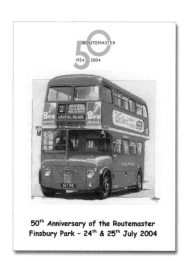

50th Anniversary of the Routemaster
Finsbury Park – 24th & 25th July 2004

A souvenir programme was available to all visitors and entrants to the event.

Routemaster Association
President Colin Curtis, OBE.

Mayor of Haringey,
Councillor Sheila Peacock.

Dr David Quarmby CBE, patron of
the Routemaster 50 event with
Colin Curtis OBE, Chair of RM50
organising committee.

The Routemaster 50 event was organised by the
Routemaster Operators and Owners Association.
Colin Curtis OBE, former chief engineer of London
Buses, Honorary President of the Routemaster
Association and former member of the
Routemaster design team, volunteered to chair the
organising sub-Committee.

Over 2½ years in the planning, many miracles were
achieved to enable vehicles to attend from not only
the British Isles but also from various parts of
Europe. Numerous vehicles were restored,
repainted, just made roadworthy, or all these feats
combined, for this significant anniversary.

RCL2223 - the commentary bus for the event.

RMC1453 - the first production RMC - the rally control bus.

3. MOUNTAINS CLIMBED

After a great deal of time and effort this team saw RM7 back on the road for the first time in 18 years.

RM506 underwent restoration at the Aston Manor Transport Museum in Birmingham and was completed for the event.

RM912 and the rebuild from heavily cannibalised condition had just begun.

RM912 returns to the Isle of Wight after travelling to the event.

RMC1485 - probably the furthest travelled in the UK, from Edinburgh.

London Central's Scania engined RM9.

RM10 star of the 102 Dalmations film.

RM44 represented the later style of livery for Routemaster operations in Southend.

The infamous RM 254 - a garage showbus since 1981 and privately preserved since 1985.

This was the last appearance of RM275 in this promotional livery for the film 'Harry Potter and the Prisoner of Azkaban'.

RM298 returned to London after service in Scotland and Manchester.

RM613 had left regular service with Stagecoach in London in August 2003, but had recently seen use on the last day of Routemaster on route 7.

RM1000 – as it says – the 1000th Routemaster built.

RM1101 from Wirral Transport Museum, Birkenhead.

A survivor - RM1368 was a 1973 fire victim that became a Chiswick test vehicle.

RM1414 made a rare return to London from the Manchester Museum of Transport.

Past Time Buses' RM1859 retains Reading Mainline style Livery.

RM2023 last saw service with MTL London in March 1998.

RM1562 is uniquely fitted with a Euro III Cummins engine.

RMC1477 resplendent in original condition, although 13 years previously it was in use as a campaign bus by Greenpeace.

RCL2220, originally a Green Line coach now in the private hire fleet with Ensignbus.

RCL2240 appeared in promotional livery for Charles Wells Brewery.

RML880 carrying RM50 logo. This was the first RML built.

RML885 appeared on the Saturday en-route to its new home with its new owner in Yorkshire.

RM16 - the lowest surviving numbered production Routemaster with a Leyland engine - with RML903 - the highest numbered 1961 RML.

Withdrawn by Metroline in March 2004 and now in the Timebus Travel fleet.

RML2665 displays the corporate livery of Stagecoach Holdings.

Representing the early 1990's refurbishment is RML2701, that travelled to the event from Wigan.

RME1 - rebuilt from RMA29 to be the longest RMA and now works with Shaftesbury & District in Dorset.

RM1 passing the line-up.

RM655 leaving the site for the journey home to Leicester.

RM1650 restored cosmetically to Silver Jubilee livery as SRM3.

RM999 passing admiring public.

RM3 was returned to original style front for the RM50 event and unveiled at 1pm, Saturday 24th.
RM3 was officially numbered RML3 to indicate a Leyland engine.

From the 1920's - K424.

From the 1930's - STL2377.

From the 1940's onwards - RT2177.

From the 1950's - and the first 8ft wide buses - RTW29.

Left to right – RT2177, RTL139, RTW29, RM1 and the last Routemaster to be built RML2760.

RM809 returned from Sweden for the event and operated on route X50.

Greene Lane's RMC1469 on route X50.

First London's RMC1510 on route 259.

RM1650 repainted back to Silver Jubilee livery as SRM3 on route 259.

Stagecoach London's RML2456 in original style County Area livery on route X50.

The unique front entrance FRM1 on route X50.

(JULY '04)

Route 19 saw two specially liveried Routemasters operating alongside their regular allocation of RMs and RMLs.

RM1.

RML3 and RM1.

RML3 and RMC4.

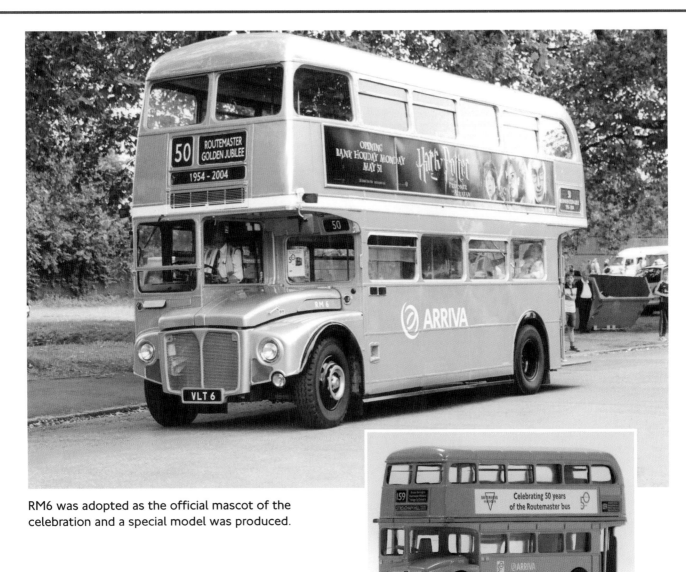

RM6 was adopted as the official mascot of the celebration and a special model was produced.

RM470 returned from Germany, especially for the event.

RMF1254, after 24 years undergoing restoration, made its debut at RM50.

RML2760, the last Routemaster built.

FRM1, the sole front entrance, rear engined Routemaster.

RMs 5 - 10, were lined up at the end of the second day.

AND WHAT ELSE TOOK PLACE DURING THE EVENT

The bus pull was won by the Queens Motors team.

It's showtime! RM254.

Queens Motors bus turnover recovery demonstration.

Precision parking taken to new limits using a laser spirit level. Jeff Stoute at work.

11. ABSENT FRIENDS

The missing prototype - London's Transport Museum's RM2 remained at Acton Depot.

Routemaster celebrations by the Bus & Truck Museum at Tempe in Australia - with RM1708.

All cameras point towards RML3.

RM50 logo is carried by RML2387 at Battersea Garage.

14. SPONSORS

Thanks to:

The Routemaster 50 event would not have been possible without the assistance of numerous people. So on behalf of all of us at the Routemaster Association, many thanks to the following people and organisations:

Steve Baker, Mark Beckham, David Bosher, Colin Curtis OBE, Lee Davis (on behalf of Arriva London), Chris Dobbing, Go-Ahead London, Alan and Barbara Gregory, Charles Howard, Mike Knight, Brian Lewer, John Lewis, London Bus Preservation Trust, Rod Lucas, Graham Lunn, Graham McQueen, Andrew Morgan (and Timothy and Laura Morgan for helping measure out window rubber for members !), Steve Morrey, Ian Rushby (and his son), Dr David Quarmby CBE, Cllr Sheila Peacock (on behalf of the London Borough of Haringey), Jeff Stoute, Chris and Ronan Sullivan, Mick and Julie Walsh, George Watson, Phil Willson, Jack Warner, Steven Wood, Richard and Robert Zarywacz, as well as numerous wives and families, and finally London's Transport Museum, as without RM1, the event would have been missing something rather special.

Apologies to anyone we have forgotten or whose names we do not know, but thanks are extended to everyone that was involved in a small or large way.

Photographs supplied by: John O'Donnell, Phillip Higgs, Mike Hurley, Mark Kehoe, Eddie Knorn, Colin Lloyd, Steve Maskell, Doreen Massey, Andrew Morgan, David Patrick, Ian Rivett, George Watson, Matthew Wharmby, and Phil Willson.

RM	Registration Number	Livery	Entrant Name / Details
RM 1	SLT 56	London Transport	London's Transport Museum, London
RML 3	SLT 58	London Transport	London Bus Preservation Trust, Cobham, Surrey
RMC 4	SLT 59	Green Line	Michael Selt, Colchester, Essex
RM 5	VLT 5	London Transport	Arriva London, London
RM 6	VLT 6	Arriva London (gold)	Arriva London, London
RM 7	VLT 7	London Transport	Mike Hurley, Goole, East Yorkshire
RM 8	VLT 8	London Transport	RM 8 Club, Sidcup, Kent
RM 9	VLT 9	London Transport	London General, London
RM 10	XFF 258	102 Dalmatians	Andy Boath, Hanwell, London
RM 16	VLT 16	London Regional Transport	Brian Lewer, Watford, Herts.
RM 24	VLT 24	London Transport	Route Twenty Four, Ferndown, Dorset
RM 44	VLT 44	Southend Transport	Stuart Miles, Benfleet, Essex
RM 120	SSL 809	First London	First Group plc, London
RM 158	VLT 158	London Transport	Robert Taylor, Great Yarmouth, Norfolk
RM 254	WLT254	London Transport	Geoff Rixon, East Molesey, Surrey
RM 275	859 UXC	Harry Potter	Arriva London, London
RM 298	VLT 298	Blue Triangle	Blue Triangle Buses, Rainham, Essex
RM 349	WLT 349	London Transport	Dave Good, Croydon, Surrey
RM 428	WLT 428	Imperial Bus Company	Imperial Bus Company, Rainham, Essex
RM 450	WLT 450	Timebus Travel	Timebus Travel, St. Albans, Herts.
RM 470	D-HF1H	Red	Herman Herfurtner, Neuss, Germany
RM 471	KVS 601	London Transport	Dr Chris Dobbing, Peterborough, Northants.
RM 506	WLT 506	London Transport	Aston Manor Transport Museum, Birmingham, West Midlands
RM 529	WLT 529	London Transport	Mike Dare, Caversham, Berks.
RM 613	WLT 613	Stagecoach East London	Nick Agnew, London
RM 642	WLT 642	London Transport	Pete Simmonds, Morden, Surrey
RM 655	WLT 655	Confidence Buses	Ken Williams, Oadby, Leics.
RM 737	WLT 737	London Transport	RM737 Group, Harrow, Middlesex
RM 765	WLT 765	London Transport	Ian Townsend, Newark, Notts
RM 795	WLT 795	Red	Mike Dawes, Ashford, Kent
RM 809	HWU 935	Red	Routemaster Travel, Vaxjo, Sweden
ER 880	WLT 880	London United	London United, London
RML 885	WLT 885	First London	Mike Mitchell, Huddersfield, Yorkshire
RML 900	WLT 900	Blue Triangle	Blue Triangle Buses, Rainham, Essex
RML 903	WLT 903	London Northern	Metroline London Northern, London
RM 912	WLT 912	London Transport	Ronan Sullivan, Shanklin, Isle of Wight
RM 938	WLT 938	London Transport	Ian Hoskin, Mitcham, Surrey
RM 980	USK 625	Stagecoach London	Peter Warrener, Winchester, Hants
RM 999	WVS 423	Reading Heritage Travel	Mike Russell, Reading, Berks.
RM 1000	100 BXL	London Transport	F. Soper, Croydon, Surrey
RM 1001	1 CLT	London Transport	Michael Smith, Billericay, Essex
RM 1101	101 CLT	Purple / Gold	Wirral Transport Museum, Birkenhead, Merseyside
RM 1224	UYJ 654	Red / Stagecoach	Mick Liddle, Colindale, London
RMF 1254	254 CLT	Imperial Bus Company	Imperial Bus Company, Rainham, Essex
RM 1274	LDS 67 A	London Transport	Ian McGregor, Hassocks, West Sussex
RM 1368	368 CLT	London Transport	Andrew Morgan, St. Albans, Herts.
RM 1397	LXU 397	London Transport	David Collins, Sutton Coldfield, West Midlands
RM 1414	414 CLT	London Transport	Greater Manchester Transport Society, Manchester
RMC 1453	453 CLT	Arriva London	Arriva London, London
RMC 1456	LFF 875	East London	John Arundell, Bagshot, Surrey
RMC 1459	459 CLT	London Country (NBC)	Paul Almeroth, Romford, Essex
RMC 1461	461 CLT	Green Line	London Bus Preservation Trust, Cobham, Surrey
RMC 1469	469 CLT	Greene Lane	Paul Wheeler, Newport, Isle of Wight

RMC 1476	476 CLT	London Country (NBC)	Clive Warneford, Gillingham, Dorset
RMC 1477	477 CLT	Green Line	Harry Hobson, Royston, Herts
RMC 1485	485 CLT	Mac Tours	Lothian Buses plc, Edinburgh, Scotland
RMC 1507	507 CLT	Green Line	Bob Humphreys, Dagenham, Essex
RMC 1510	510 CLT	First London	First Group plc, London
RMC 1513	513 CLT	Metroline	Metroline London Northern, London
RM 1562	562 CLT	Sovereign	London Sovereign, Edgware, Middlesex
RM 1641	641 DYE	Imperial Bus Company	Imperial Bus Company, Rainham, Essex
RM 1650	650 DYE	Silver Jubilee (SRM 3)	First Group plc, London
RM 1699	699 DYE	London Transport	Steven Wood, Hertford, Herts
RM 1804	804 DYE	MTL London	Paul Watson, Cheam, Surrey
RM 1859	859 DYE	Past Time Buses	Past Time Buses, Reading, Berks
RM 1871	ALD 871 B	Timebus Travel	Timebus Travel, St. Albans, Herts
RM 1989	ALD 989 B	Blackpool Transport	Brian Lilley, Tilehurst, Berks
RM 1990	ALD 990 B	Reading Mainline	Shaun Bradbury, Reading, Berks
RM 2023	ALM 23 B	MTL London	Trevor Little, Hounslow, Middlesex
RM 2037	ALM 37 B	London Transport	Keith Rose, Staines, Surrey
RM 2097	ALM 97 B	London Buses	Tim Barrington, Isleworth, Middlesex
RM 2107	CUV 107C	Red	International Coaches, Thornton Heath, Surrey
RM 2116	CUV 116 C	1983 Golden Jubilee	Graham Lunn, Egham, Surrey
RM 2180	CUV 180 C	London Transport	Martin Clitheroe, Bromley, Kent
RM 2213	CUV 213 C	London Transport	Yossarian Gay, Southampton, Hants
RM 2217	CUV 217 C	Arriva London	Arriva London, London
RCL 2220	CUV 220 C	Ensignbus (red)	Ensignbus, Purfleet, Essex
RCL 2223	CUV 223 C	Red	British Airports Authority, Heathrow, Middlesex
RCL 2229	CUV 229 C	Green Line	London's Transport Museum, London
RCL 2233	CUV 233 C	Green Line	Alan Brown, Romford, Essex
RCL 2240	CUV 240 C	Charles Wells Advert	Charles Wells Ltd., Bedford, Beds
RML 2299	CUV 299 C	Metroline	Geoffrey Emslie, London
RML 2310	CUV 310 C	Timebus Travel	Timebus Travel, St. Albans, Herts
RML 2317	CUV 317 C	Metrobus (green)	Metrobus Ltd., Crawley, West Sussex
RML 2419	CUV 419 C	Under restoration	Lee Rose, London Colney, Herts
RML 2445	JJD 445D	Red	London Classic Bus Hire, Greenhithe, Kent
RML 2446	JJD 446D	Under restoration	Richard Mercer, Potters Bar, Herts
RML 2456	JJD 456 D	London Country	Stagecoach London, London
RML 2579	JJD 579 D	Bus Red	Gwilym Owen, London
RML 2620	NML 620 E	Metroline	Dave Good, Croydon, Surrey
RML 2665	SMK 665 F	Stagecoach corporate	Stagecoach London, London
RML 2699	SMK 699 F	London Buses	Austin Blackburn, Orpington, Kent
RML 2701	SMK 701 F	Metroline	David Dawber & Gareth Hughes, Wigan, Lancs
RML 2735	SMK 735 F	First London	First Group plc, London
RML 2755	SMK 755 F	Metroline	Liam Doyle, Willesden, London
RML 2760	SMK 760 F	London Transport	Stagecoach London, London
FRM 1	KGY 4 D	London Transport	London's Transport Museum, London
RME 1	KGJ 603 D	Shaftesbury & District (red)	Shaftesbury & District, Motcombe, Dorset
K 424	XC 8059	General	London's Transport Museum, London
T 31	UU 6646	General	London Bus Preservation Trust, Cobham, Surrey
T 219	GK 5486	Green Line	London's Transport Museum, London
STL 2377	EGO 426	London Transport	London Bus Preservation Trust, Cobham, Surrey
T 504	EPL 228	London Transport	London Bus Preservation Trust, Cobham, Surrey
RT 2177	KGU 106	London Transport	John Herting, Chorleywood, Herts
RTL 139	KGK 803	London Transport	London Bus Preservation Trust, Cobham, Surrey
RTW 29	KGK 529	London Transport	Roy Adams, Bristol, Avon
RF 366	MXX 8	London Transport	Jim Andress, Chippenham, Wilts